GETTING TO KNOW THE WORLD'S GREATEST ARTISTS

FREDERIC
REMINGTON

WRITTEN AND ILLUSTRATED BY MIKE VENEZIA

CHILDREN'S PRESS®
A DIVISION OF SCHOLASTIC INC.
NEW YORK TORONTO LONDON AUCKLAND SYDNEY
MEXICO CITY NEW DELHI HONG KONG
DANBURY, CONNECTICUT

Dedication: To Naomi Rebecca, from your Uncle Mike

Cover: *The Cowboy,* by Frederic Remington. 1902, oil on canvas, 40 1/4 x 27 1/8 in.
© Amon Carter Museum, Fort Worth, Texas, 1961.382.

Colorist for illustrations: Dave Ludwig

Library of Congress Cataloging-in-Publication Data

Venezia, Mike.
  Frederic Remington / written and illustrated by Mike Venezia.
    p. cm. — (Getting to know the world's greatest artists)
Summary: Describes the life and career of the late nineteenth-century
and early twentieth-century artist who is best known for his paintings
and sculptures of the American West.
  ISBN 0-516-22497-2 (lib. bdg.)   0-516-27812-6 (pbk.)
  1. Remington, Frederic, 1861-1909—Juvenile literature. 2.
Artists—United States—Biography—Juvenile literature. 3. West
(U.S.)—In art—Juvenile literature. [1. Remington, Frederic, 1861-1909.
2. Artists.] I. Remington, Frederic, 1861-1909. II. Title.
  N6537.R4 V46 2002
  709'.2—dc21

                              2002001607

CHILDREN'S PRESS and associated logos are trademarks and or registered
trademarks of Grolier Publishing Co., Inc. SCHOLASTIC and associated
logos are trademarks and or registered trademarks of Scholastic Inc.

1 2 3 4 5 6 7 8 9 10 R 11 10 09 08 07 06 05 04 03 02

Self-Portrait on a Horse,
by Frederic Remington. 1890,
oil on canvas, 29 3/16 x 18 3/8 in.
© Sid Richardson Collection of
Western Art, Fort Worth, TX.

Frederic Remington was born in Canton, New York, in 1861. Even though he grew up and lived in the busy eastern part of the United States, he is known for his exciting pictures of America's Wild West.

Through the Smoke Sprang the Daring Soldier, by Frederic Remington. 1897, oil on canvas, 27 1/4 x 40 in.
© Amon Carter Museum, Fort Worth, Texas, 1961.243.

In the 1800s, thousands of people from large towns and cities moved out West in hopes of finding a better life. Frederic Remington often traveled out West to get ideas for his favorite scenes. These were usually action-packed

On the Southern Plains, by Frederic Remington. 1907, oil on canvas, 30 1/8 x 51 1/8 in.
© Metropolitan Museum of Art, Gift of Several Gentlemen, 1911, (11.192).

pictures of battles and fights between cowboys, American Indians, and the United States Cavalry.

Frederic especially loved to paint running horses—the faster, the better!

Sometimes Remington showed a rugged cowboy taming a bucking bronco, or outlaws about to hold up a stagecoach. Even when everything seems very still, Frederic Remington's pictures can make you wonder what will happen next.

A Cold Morning on the Range, by Frederic Remington. ca. 1904, oil on canvas, 27 x 40 in.
© Christie's Images, The Anschutz Collection, Denver, CO.

The Questionable Companionship (The Parley), by Frederic Remington. ca. 1903, oil on canvas, 68.5 x 102 cm.
© Thyssen-Bornemisza Collection, Lugano, Switzerland.

In the painting above, you can't be sure whether the two men will trust each other and become friends or end up fighting. In these paintings, Frederic Remington lets your imagination create the action.

Frederic's mother remembered that when her son was very little, he spent hours drawing pictures with chalk on a piece of slate. As he grew up, Frederic was known as a troublemaker by the grown-ups in his town. He and his friends were always pulling one prank or another.

Frederic didn't do very well in school, except in sports and drawing. This worried his father, Colonel Remington. Colonel Remington hoped his son would become a military officer. He knew that unless Frederic earned good grades, this would never happen.

Frederic Remington admired his father more than anyone. Colonel Remington was a brave Civil War hero. Aside from being loving and understanding, the colonel taught his son to ride and appreciate horses.

He told Frederic many stories of his
exciting war adventures, too. During his
high-school years, Frederic did go to a military
academy, but his heart wasn't in it. He was
more interested in drawing soldiers than in
becoming one.

After high school, Frederic's parents pretty much gave up on the idea of their son having a military career. They agreed to let Frederic enter the art department at Yale University. Frederic didn't enjoy his art classes there very much, though. He was much too restless to sit in a room copying plaster statues all day.

Remington (front row, far right) with Yale football team. 1879.
© Frederic Remington Art Museum, Ogdensburg, New York.

A Run Behind Interference, Harper's Weekly, 12/2/1893, p. 1152, by Frederic Remington. 1893, halftone illustration. © HarpWeek, LLC.

Frederic spent most of his time at Yale playing football on their championship team. In the 1870s, football was much more dangerous than it is today. Players used hardly any protective equipment and there were lots of injuries. But Frederic was never worried. He loved the excitement of the game and became a team hero.

The Rocky Mountains, Lander's Peak, by Albert Bierstadt. 1863, oil on canvas, 73 1/2 x 120 3/4 in. © Metropolitan Museum of Art, Rogers Fund, 1907, (07.123), photograph by Schecter Lee.

Frederic went to Yale for only a short time. During Frederic's second year, Colonel Remington became seriously ill. Frederic returned home to be with his father. Soon after Frederic arrived, Colonel Remington died. This was the saddest moment of Frederic Remington's life.

WEST.

FINIS.

For the next few months, Frederic forgot about art. He tried out different jobs, but none of them worked out very well. Frederic decided then to take a trip out West. This was something he had always dreamed about. When he was in military school, Frederic had drawn a picture of himself heading west.

In 1881, when Frederic was twenty years old, he left home for the Montana Territory. This was probably the most important trip of his life. One night, while sitting around a campfire, Frederic met an old wagon driver. The old man told stories of how he had seen the Wild West quickly changing.

He told Frederic that it wouldn't be long
before there would be lots of people and
buildings all over the place. Frederic
Remington said he decided right then and
there to do all he could to record the Wild
West before it disappeared forever!

One of the first things Frederic did was draw a picture of a group of cowboys being warned of danger. Since he didn't bring any art supplies with him, he drew his picture on an old, wrinkled piece of wrapping paper. Frederic mailed his drawing to a well-known magazine in New York City called *Harper's Weekly*.

Cowboys of Arizona - Roused by a Scout, Harper's Weekly, 2/25/1882, by Frederic Remington.
1882, magazine cover, halftone, 16 x 11 1/4 in. © HarpWeek, LLC.

Surprisingly, the editor of the magazine liked Frederic's illustration. Because it was roughly drawn, the editor had a professional artist redraw it. Frederic's first illustration was printed in *Harper's Weekly* in 1882!

The Unknown Explorers, Collier's Weekly,
8/11/1906, by Frederic Remington.
1906, color halftone print, 7 1/4 x 5 in.
© Frederic Remington Art Museum,
Ogdensburg, New York.

Remington Number, Collier's Weekly, 3/18/1905,
by Frederic Remington. 1905, magazine cover,
16 x 11 in. © Frederic Remington Art Museum,
Ogdensburg, New York.

Frederic Remington came along at just
the right time to be an illustrator. In the late
1800s, people used magazines the way they
use television, radio, and movies today.
People in big, crowded cities couldn't wait
to read weekly stories by their favorite authors.

The Rescue of Corporal Scott, Harper's Weekly, 8/21/1886, by Frederic Remington. 1886, magazine cover, 16 x 11 1/4 in. © HarpWeek, LLC.

They especially loved illustrated adventures of the Wild West.

Remington decided to see if he could make a living from his artwork. He worked hard to improve his drawing skills. Within a few years, he became one of the most popular illustrators in the United States.

He did all kinds of illustrations for stories about the Indian wars and the lives of settlers and cowboys. Frederic was a fun person to be around. He loved parties and telling jokes. Because of this, he never had any trouble interviewing cowboys or talking them into being models.

A Cavalryman's Breakfast on the Plains, by Frederic Remington. ca. 1892, oil on canvas, 22 1/8 x 32 1/8 in. © Amon Carter Museum, Fort Worth, Texas, 1961.227.

Marching in the Desert, by Frederic Remington. 1888, engraved illustration, 5 x 8.
© Frederic Remington Art Museum, Ogdensburg, New York.

The U.S. Army was always glad to have
Frederic along during scouting missions.
These missions helped keep the peace on
the frontier. In the painting above, Frederic
included himself with the famous Buffalo
Soldiers. He's the second one in line.
Sometimes Frederic wrote his own stories
to go along with his illustrations.

Aiding a Comrade (Past All Surgery), by Frederic Remington. 1889-1890, oil on canvas, 34 x 48 1/8 in.
© Museum of Fine Arts, Houston, The Hogg Brothers Collection, gift of Miss Ima Hogg.

Over the years, some people have had problems with the way Frederic Remington showed American Indians in his paintings. Frederic was like many settlers at that time who believed that American Indians were dangerous warriors. People from big cities in the East felt that Indians stood in the way of making the West a place to build new cities, raise cattle, and search for gold. The settlers

The Snow Trail, by Frederic Remington. 1908, oil on canvas, 27 x 40 in.
© Frederic Remington Art Museum, Ogdensburg, New York.

didn't care that the land they were taking belonged to the American Indians.

Remington often showed American Indians causing problems, even though these people were just trying to protect their land and villages. Later in his life, though, Frederic Remington began to respect the Indians' way of life and showed them as proud people.

A Dash for the Timber, by Frederic Remington. 1889, oil on canvas, 48 1/4 x 84 1/8 in.
© Amon Carter Museum, Fort Worth, Texas, 1961.381.

Frederic Remington was never really in a battle or gunfight himself. When he traveled throughout the West, he sketched what he saw and listened to stories that soldiers, Indians, cowboys, and mountain men told him. He then made up scenes the way he imagined them to have happened.

Frederic collected tons of western items
to bring back to his studio in New York.
He used the things he collected to make
sure details in his paintings were as authentic
as possible.

Charge of the Rough Riders, by Frederic Remington. 1898, oil on canvas, 35 x 60 in.
© Frederic Remington Art Museum, Ogdensburg, New York.

Frederic did get pretty close to a battle once. In 1898, he was asked to illustrate soldiers fighting in Cuba during the Spanish-American War. Frederic couldn't wait to see the exciting battles of a real war. But when he got to Cuba, what he saw was a lot of wounded and dying soldiers.

This trip saddened Frederic Remington very much. It changed forever the way he felt about war. After the war was over, Frederic's friend Teddy Roosevelt asked him to make a painting showing Roosevelt leading the charge of a famous battle. Roosevelt later became president of the United States.

Frederic Remington always felt left out when it came to being accepted as a *real* artist. Many people who collected artwork for museums thought of him as just an illustrator. Near the end of his life, Frederic actually burned up many of his illustrations in a big bonfire! He then spent most of his time painting pictures that he hoped would be shown in museums someday.

A Taint on the Wind, by Frederic Remington. 1906, oil on canvas, 27 1/8 x 40 in.
© Sid Richardson Collection of Western Art, Fort Worth, TX.

In these remarkable paintings, Frederic Remington was able to make you feel details rather than see them. Today Frederic Remington's paintings and illustrations are shown in museums all over the world.

Mountain Man, by Frederic Remington. 1903, lost-wax cast bronze, 28 1/2 h x 21 w x 11 1/8 d. © Frederic Remington Art Museum, Ogdensburg, New York.

Aside from his thrilling pictures of the Wild West, Frederic Remington was known for his bronze sculptures. More than anything else, Frederic hoped he would be remembered for the way he could paint and sculpt horses. By the time Remington died in 1909, most people agreed that his horses were among the best ever.

Works of art in this book can be seen at the following places:

Amon Carter Museum, Fort Worth

Frederic Remington Art Museum, Ogdensburg

Metropolitan Museum of Art, New York

Museum of Fine Arts, Houston

Sid Richardson Collection of Western Art, Fort Worth

Thyssen-Bornemisza Collection, Lugano